Little People, **BIG DREAMS**™

AMANDA GORMAN

Written by
Maria Isabel Sánchez Vegara

Illustrated by
Queenbe Monyei

Frances Lincoln
Children's Books

Little Amanda lived with her mother and sisters in a two-bedroom apartment in Los Angeles. She had trouble pronouncing some letters, but that didn't stop her from loving words like *plum*, *stone*, and *spoon*.

Amanda read everything, from books to cereal boxes.
She kept a diary and even tried writing her own dictionary!
One day, while listening to her teacher read poetry,
Amanda decided to become a poet.

Having a speech impediment was a hill to climb for a poet, but Amanda saw it as a gift. Practicing her words with a song full of R's and going to speech therapy made her feel stronger and better.

She was a teenager when she set her eyes on a special book.
A Black girl was staring at her from its cover, and it was written by
an African-American woman. Looking at it, Amanda realized that
all the books she had read before were written by white men.

Discovering books written by authors who looked like her helped Amanda find her own voice. She was the daughter of Black writers, descended from freedom fighters who broke their chains and changed the world.

The first time she stepped up to the mic was at a poetry workshop. Amanda was worried about how her voice would sound.

But once she started performing her poem, she felt
that all of her ancestors were right next to her.

From the lyrics in a song to the signs of protesters on the streets, she saw poetry everywhere.

For Amanda, it was not just a beautiful form of art,
but a tool to change the world.

She decided to study sociology, the science that explores how humans behave in groups. Amanda was a sophomore in Harvard when she was named America's first Youth Poet Laureate, which led her to perform all around the country.

When Joe Biden was chosen to be the next President of the United States, he asked Amanda to read a poem at his swearing-in ceremony. She couldn't wait to run home and tell her twin sister. She was about to follow in the steps of one of her favorite poets, Maya Angelou.

Do the best you can until you know better. When you know better, do better.

–Maya Angelou

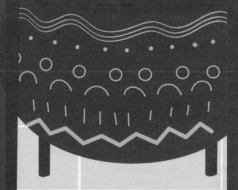

The night before, Amanda rehearsed her poem over and over in front of the mirror. The country had lived moments of great division, and she just hoped for two things: bringing a message of unity and not tripping on her way to the podium.

The whole world was moved by her poem! Amanda's words invited everyone to lay down their arms and hold hands to build a better country; a country where a skinny Black girl could dream of becoming its president.

NEW WORDS

ABILITY

BRILLIANT

OBSERVE

EXPLORE

on of **Joseph R.**

Amanda kept writing about diversity, justice, and equality; things that were bigger than herself. Her books became instant best-sellers, her articles the most read, and her presence a shining light for others.

And there will be many more words to add to little Amanda's story, like **step**, *first*, and **high**. Because, as she once wrote, "Every day, we write the future."

AMANDA GORMAN

(Born 1998)

c. 2018

2018

Amanda Gorman was born in Los Angeles, California, on March 7th 1998. Her and her two sisters were encouraged by their mom, an English teacher, to spend time reading and writing. As a small child, Amanda was diagnosed with an auditory processing disorder and a speech impediment, but she saw them both as a gift that would be her strength. She fell in love with poetry at school after hearing her teacher read aloud in class. As a teenager, she was inspired after discovering a book by Toni Morrison, and realized that her voice as a Black woman was too important to be silenced. In 2014, she became the Los Angeles Youth Poet Laureate, and in 2015, she published her first book, *The One for Whom Food is Not Enough*. As a student, she was named America's first ever National Youth Poet Laureate.

2020   2021

This honor saw her perform at events across the country, and during an event at the Library of Congress, future First Lady Jill Biden heard her speak. Three years later, at President Joe Biden's inauguration on January 20th 2021, Amanda became the youngest ever inaugural poet at the age of 22. Stood in front of the US Capitol building, she recited her poem, "The Hill We Climb," about her hope for a brighter future for America. It was a groundbreaking moment that inspired millions of people watching across the world. Her books shot to the top of the best-sellers list, and she became the first poet to ever feature on the cover of *Vogue* magazine. A beacon of light for dreamers everywhere, Amanda's words and spirit remind us that we are more powerful together than we are apart.

Want to find out more about **Amanda Gorman?**

Have a read of this great book:

Change Sings: A Children's Anthem

by Amanda Gorman

Brimming with creative inspiration, how-to projects, and useful information to enrich your everyday life, Quarto Knows is a favourite destination for those pursuing their interests and passions. Visit our site and dig deeper with our books into your area of interest: Quarto Creates, Quarto Cooks, Quarto Homes, Quarto Lives, Quarto Drives, Quarto Explores, Quarto Gifts, or Quarto Kids.

Text © 2022 Maria Isabel Sánchez Vegara. Illustrations © 2022 Queenbe Monyei.

Original concept of the series by Maria Isabel Sánchez Vegara, published by Alba Editorial, s.l.u

Little People Big Dreams and Pequeña&Grande are registered trademarks of Alba Editorial, s.l.u. for books, printed publications, e-books and audiobooks. Produced under licence from Alba Editorial, s.l.u.

First Published in the USA in 2021 by Frances Lincoln Children's Books, an imprint of The Quarto Group.

Quarto Boston North Shore, 100 Cummings Center, Suite 265D, Beverly, MA 01915, USA

Tel: +1 978-282-9590, Fax: +1 978-283-2742 **www.QuartoKnows.com**

A catalogue record for this book is available from the British Library.

ISBN 978-0-7112-7071-8

Set in Futura BT.

Published by Katie Cotton • Designed by Lyli Feng

Edited by Lucy Menzies • Production by Nikki Ingram

Editorial Assistance from Rachel Robinson

Manufactured in Guangdong, China CC112021

1 3 5 7 9 8 6 4 2

Photographic acknowledgements (pages 28-29, from left to right): 1. Amanda Gorman speaks onstage at Girlboss Rally NYC 2018 at Knockdown Center on November 18, 2018 in Maspeth, New York. © JP Yim/Stringer via Getty Images. 2. Amanda Gorman attends the Black Girls Rock! 2018 Red Carpet at NJPAC on August 26, 2018 in Newark, New Jersey. © Dave Kotinsky/Stringer via Getty Images. 3. Amanda Gorman attends the American Black Film Festival Honors Awards Ceremony at The Beverly Hilton Hotel on February 23, 2020 in Beverly Hills, California. © Amy Sussman/Staff via Getty Images. 4. American poet Amanda Gorman reads a poem during the 59th presidential inauguration in Washington, D.C., U.S., on Wednesday, Jan. 20, 2021. © Patrick Semansky/AP Photo/Bloomberg via Getty Images

Collect the Little People, BIG DREAMS™ series:

FRIDA KAHLO	COCO CHANEL	MAYA ANGELOU	AMELIA EARHART	AGATHA CHRISTIE	MARIE CURIE	ROSA PARKS	AUDREY HEPBURN
EMMELINE PANKHURST	ELLA FITZGERALD	ADA LOVELACE	JANE AUSTEN	GEORGIA O'KEEFFE	HARRIET TUBMAN	ANNE FRANK	MOTHER TERESA
JOSEPHINE BAKER	L. M. MONTGOMERY	JANE GOODALL	SIMONE DE BEAUVOIR	MUHAMMAD ALI	STEPHEN HAWKING	MARIA MONTESSORI	VIVIENNE WESTWOOD
MAHATMA GANDHI	DAVID BOWIE	WILMA RUDOLPH	DOLLY PARTON	BRUCE LEE	RUDOLF NUREYEV	ZAHA HADID	MARY SHELLEY
MARTIN LUTHER KING JR.	DAVID ATTENBOROUGH	ASTRID LINDGREN	EVONNE GOOLAGONG	BOB DYLAN	ALAN TURING	BILLIE JEAN KING	GRETA THUNBERG
JESSE OWENS	JEAN-MICHEL BASQUIAT	ARETHA FRANKLIN	CORAZON AQUINO	PELÉ	ERNEST SHACKLETON	STEVE JOBS	AYRTON SENNA
LOUISE BOURGEOIS	ELTON JOHN	JOHN LENNON	PRINCE	CHARLES DARWIN	CAPTAIN TOM MOORE	HANS CHRISTIAN ANDERSEN	STEVIE WONDER

MEGAN RAPINOE · MARY ANNING · MALALA YOUSAFZAI · ANDY WARHOL · RUPAUL · MICHELLE OBAMA · MINDY KALING · IRIS APFEL

ROSALIND FRANKLIN · RUTH BADER GINSBURG · MARILYN MONROE · KAMALA HARRIS · ALBERT EINSTEIN · CHARLES DICKENS · YOKO ONO · MICHAEL JORDAN

NELSON MANDELA · PABLO PICASSO · AMANDA GORMAN · GLORIA STEINEM · FLORENCE NIGHTINGALE · HARRY HOUDINI · J.R.R. TOLKIEN

ACTIVITY BOOKS

STICKER ACTIVITY BOOK · COLORING BOOK · LITTLE ME, BIG DREAMS JOURNAL

Discover more about the series at www.littlepeoplebigdreams.com